iPlayMusic.com

Beginner Guitar Lessons
Learn the Quick, Simple, and Easy Way

iPlayMusic, Inc.

For more information about iPlayMusic, Inc., please email us at sales@iplaymusic.com.

www.iPlayMusic.com

ISBN 0-9760487-3-6

Introduction

The vision of iPlayMusic, Inc. is to teach people how to play their favorite songs on their favorite musical instruments. In *Beginner Guitar Lessons* we present the essentials you need to know in order to start playing songs right away.

iPlayMusic, Inc. was formed by three friends who share a passion for music and instruction. We have 20 years combined playing experience and have studied music formally at Musician's Institute (GIT) and the university level.

In developing our teaching method, we conducted extensive research – we spoke to friends, other instructors, advanced players, beginners, and people who always wanted to play a musical instrument but hadn't even taken the first step. In this process we quickly learned that most people quit playing guitar because they get frustrated with traditional teaching methods and don't find the process enjoyable.

The key reasons we found were that books, videos and even personal instructors typically focus the first few lessons on guitar theory, scales, notation and other topics that can be confusing and frustrating for beginners. Based on this research, we decided to focus on teaching people the skills they need to play songs as soon as possible.

Playing guitar is a skill you will enjoy the rest of your life. It can be a way to escape the mundane, give joy to others, or simply have fun and relax. We hope you will pick up skills from this book that will help you learn guitar and the songs you love.

Sincerely,

Quincy, Scott, Mike, and Jen
The iPlayMusic Team

How to Use the Book and DVD

This book is designed to be used in combination with the accompanying DVD. For sections where we have included video, you should read through that section and any prior sections first before watching the videos. When you are ready to watch the videos, simply place the DVD into any DVD player and either press play to watch from beginning to end or navigate through each section to watch a particular video.

This book is written for the beginning student. Each section builds upon the previous sections, so it is very important to take a **step-by-step** approach.

If you approach the lessons this way, by the end you will have mastered the fundamentals that will enable you to play songs effortlessly.

So, if you're ready to start playing music, let's get started!

Beginner Guitar Lessons
Learn the Quick, Simple, and Easy Way

Contents

Page

Beginner Guitar Volume 1: Basics

Contents (cont'd)

Beginner Guitar Volume 1: Basics

1. Guitar Anatomy

Before we get into the lessons, it is important to understand some basic terminology and the layout of your guitar. The anatomy of the guitar is organized much like the human body:

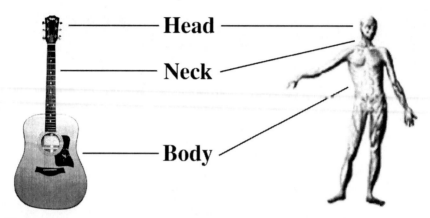

Head

Neck

Body

Figure 1

Guitar Head

This is the part of the guitar that has the knobs (called tuning keys) that you use to tune your guitar.

Guitar Neck

This is the long part of the guitar that the strings run across. The front of the neck is called the **fretboard**.

Guitar Body

This is the largest part of the guitar. If you have an **acoustic guitar** or hollow body **electric guitar**, then it's the part that is hollowed out. Guitar bodies have many different shapes, sizes, and wood types that create a variety of tones. If you have an **electric guitar** with a solid body, the sound is converted to an electric signal through your guitar pickups that are located under the strings on the body of the guitar. The signal is sent to your amplifier via the guitar cable, and the amplifier then boosts the signal and adds its own character to the sound.

Guitar Frets

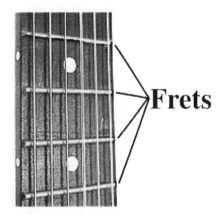

Guitar frets are the **metal strips** on the fretboard of the guitar neck. Frets are spaced apart from each other and span all the way up the neck. Frets exist so that when you press down on a string at a particular position of the neck, the string makes a specific tone. **The higher up** the neck you go, the higher the "pitch" of the sound will be.

Figure 2

Fret and String Numbering.

In this book and in the accompanying videos, we number the frets and strings for simplicity.

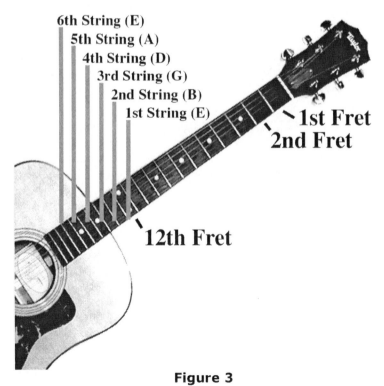

6th String (E)
5th String (A)
4th String (D)
3rd String (G)
2nd String (B)
1st String (E)

1st Fret
2nd Fret

12th Fret

Figure 3

Tuning keys

There are 6 tuning keys on the head of your guitar. By turning these keys, you can adjust the tension of the strings on the guitar. By tightening, you can raise the pitch of a particular string. By loosening, you can lower the pitch.

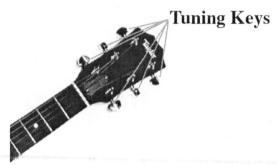

Tuning Keys

Figure 4

—Bridge

Guitar Bridge

The bridge is located at the base of the guitar body. It holds the end of the strings to the guitar on the body.

Figure 5

For the best (most resonant) tone, the strings of the guitar should be strummed in between the base of the neck of the guitar and the bridge of the guitar (the boxed area).

These are the essential parts of the guitar that we will be discussing in this book. There is a lot of other guitar-specific and musical terminology that we've chosen to omit, simply because we want to keep things as simple and straight forward as possible, so you can start having fun and playing right away.

2. How to hold your Guitar

Body Positioning

First, find a comfortable place to sit where you can have your legs in front of you and your feet on the ground. This is your **"foundation"** that the guitar will rest on.

Next, make sure you're sitting comfortably and have good posture.

Figure 6

Playing guitar for hours will eventually strain your back if you do not maintain a nice **upright** sitting posture. Pick up your guitar and place the back of the guitar against your stomach. If you are **right handed**, the guitar neck should be pointing towards your left. Rest the guitar body on your right thigh.

Now place your left hand around the guitar neck and place your right arm around the body so that your hand is lying by the strings. Adjust your body positioning as necessary, so that you are completely comfortable.

Hand Positioning

If you're **left handed**, don't worry, Jimi Hendrix was left-handed! You basically have two options here. The first option is to buy a right-handed guitar and re-string it, so that the order of the strings in figure 3 is reversed. The second option you have is to buy a left-handed guitar.

If you're **right handed**, you will use your left hand, as shown below, to construct chords.

As you can see in Figure 7, the left hand fingers are bent and pressing down on the strings on the fretboard. The back of the neck is curved, so that your hand molds into the shape of the neck. In this image, the thumb is arching aver the top of the neck. This is a common thumb position for constructing chords.

Figure 7

It is also o.k. to press **your thumb** into the back of the guitar neck when constructing chords, although this is more common when playing scales. Try out both thumb positions and use the one that is most comfortable for you.

Figure 8

Don't worry about what strings your left-hand fingers are pressing down on at this point. We are just trying to get you familiar with the hand and finger positioning.

For the chords you will learn in this book it is very important that you have only your fingertips touching the strings. If any other part of your fingers are touching the strings when you construct a chord, it will sound muffled or muted. **To be clear**, there are many instances, such as when constructing bar chords, that it is perfectly fine, in fact desirable, to allow your entire finger to lay across the strings. However, **for the basic chords** in this lesson, it is important to only press down on the strings with your fingertips.

Right Hand/Arm

This is the hand that you will use **to "strum"** the strings to make the different chord sounds. Remember to position your hand so that when you strike the strings, you are strumming in the shaded region of figure 5. This is the most resonant sounding part of the guitar.

Figure 9

Lie your right arm over the guitar. Your **right bicep** should be resting on the top of the body of the guitar. Your **hand** should be positioned directly above the sound hole in the guitar. This is where the sound is produced. Figure 9 shows the correct right hand/arm positioning.

3. Guitar Pick

The guitar pick is used with the strumming hand to either pick the strings individually or strum them all at once to play chords. Picks come in many shapes and sizes. **The thickness** of the pick is usually marked on the pick. Thickness ranges from thin to heavy. Medium is a good thickness **to start with**, but you should try a few different gauges and see what thickness you like.

Not all guitarists use a pick. Mark Knopfler, the guitarist from Dire Straits is perhaps the most famous lead guitarist in the pop music world to use his fingers, rather than a pick, when soloing. Classical and flamenco guitarists also use fingerstyle rather than a pick to play the guitar. For the most part, it is easier for beginners to produce a nice smooth sound with the pick, so we suggest that you learn how to play with a pick first and then venture off into the world of fingerstyle once you are more advanced.

The guitar pick **is held** with the thumb and index finger of the strumming hand. Grip the fat end of the pick between your thumb and index finger. The pointed part of the pick should be facing in towards the strings. See figure 10.

Striking the strings with the pick

Now that you understand how to hold the pick, you should practice striking individual strings on the guitar. Make sure that you have a firm grip, and then strike the 6th string, making sure that you **strike the string** with the very tip of the pick (about 1/4 of the pick's surface area). In general, if you strike the strings with the same intensity, **the more tip** you have exposed the louder the chord will be. Try striking the 6th string lightly and then more firm to notice the different tones you can generate. **Avoid** striking the string so hard that it buzzes. This is a sure sign that you're picking too hard.

Figure 10

4. Tuning your Guitar

Tuning the guitar is **critical**, because nothing you play will sound "right" if the guitar is not in tune. If your guitar is out of tune or tuned incorrectly it will make a perfectly constructed chord sound bad.

There are **many ways** to tune your guitar:

1. With an electronic tuner
2. With tuning software
3. By ear with a tuning fork
4. By ear with another guitar or reference note

The easiest and most accurate way to tune your guitar is with an **electronic tuner** or with tuning software. Electronic tuners typically work for both acoustic or electric guitars, although this is not always the case. An acoustic guitar tuner will have a built in mic, to pick up the sound. Electric guitar tuners usually have a 1/4" instrument cable input for the guitar. Most tuners have both a built in mic and a 1/4" instrument cable input. We highly recommend that you purchase an electronic tuner, such as the Boss TU-15 Chromatic Tuner.

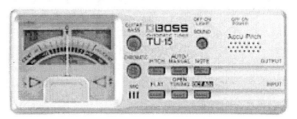

Figure 11

Figure 12

There is also some great free or inexpensive **software** available for tuning the guitar. For example, EZTuner4U is a $16 chromatic musical instrument tuner that sees your computer sound card and microphone.

Although electronic tuners and software tuners are great tools, we suggest that you learn to tune your guitar by ear to a reference note. **This will help you** to train your ear, so you can quickly tune during a live performance or when you don't have an electronic tuner nearby.

On the DVD you will find the properly tuned **notes** for each of the strings on the guitar. Play the "Tuning & String Numbering" section on the DVD now to hear the sound of each string. Try matching the pitch of your strings to these notes by adjusting the tuning keys on the head of your guitar.

You can also try tuning with **a tuning fork.** A tuning fork will provide you with a reference tone. You can purchase tuning forks at any musical instrument retailer. The most common tuning fork for guitarists generates an A (440) **reference tone**, so you can tune the 5th string (A). In order to generate a tone with the tuning fork, you should lightly tap it against a hard surface and then press the non-forked end against the body of your guitar. This will cause the tone to resonate throughout the guitar body, so that it is louder.

Tune your 5th string to the A tuning fork's tone by picking the "open" 5th (A) string ("open" means that you just play the string without pressing down on any frets) while listening to the tone of the tuning fork (you can also use the 5th string sound file provided above if you don't have a tuning fork). **Adjust the tuning key** for your 5th string by turning it in either direction until the tone of the picked string and the tuning fork are identical.

Once your 5th string is in tune, you can tune all the rest of the strings on your guitar. Start with the 6th (E) string. This is the fattest string of the six. It's also the string at the top of the guitar (See figure 3 for reference).

Press your index finger on the 5th fret, 6th string. **Make sure** that you press firmly and that your index finger is close to the edge of the fret, almost touching it. If your string is buzzing as you pick it, then either you are not pressing firmly enough, or your finger is not positioned close enough to the edge of the fret.

Pick the 6th string with your index finger pressing down on the 5th fret 6th string and then pick the "open" 5th (A) string. Compare the two tones. The pitch of the 5th fret, 6th string should be the same sound as the open 5th (A) string. If it is not the exact same sound then turn the 6th string's tuning key so that the sound is the same. Now your 6th and 5th string are tuned.

Repeat this step, but this time place your index finger on the 5th fret of the 5th string. Pick that string and then pick the open 4th string. They should sound the same. If they don't, then turn the tuning key for the 4th string so that the 4th string sounds like the 5th. Be careful to turn the correct tuning key.

Continue the same process from the 4th string to the third string. When you get to tuning the second string there is a slight change. To tune the 2nd (B) string, place your index finger on the 4th fret, 3rd string (instead of the 5th fret). Now pick the 3rd string and then pick the second string. If the second string does not sound like the third then turn the second string's tuning key so that the second string sounds like the 3rd.

Finally, for the 1st (E) string, move your index finger back to the 5th fret on the second string. Then pick the 2nd and 1st strings. The open 1st string should sound exactly like the 5th fret, 2nd string. If it doesn't then turn the 1st string's tuning key so that it sounds like the second string.

Ok that is probably going to be the toughest part of learning to play guitar. We recommend you buy an electronic tuner, but knowing how to tune the guitar by ear will be extremely valuable, especially in live playing situations or at times when you don't have access to a guitar tuner.

5. Basic Chords

Now for the fun stuff. In this section we will teach you the basic chords you need to know to play the songs you love. So let's get started!

Before we move on to chord construction, here are some **basic tips** that will help you sound better.

1. Press firmly.

Be sure you press each finger down so that it firmly presses the string against the fretboard. This will ensure the sound of the string is clean and does not buzz. If you don't push the string down hard enough you will hear a buzzing or a muffled sound.

2. Close to the fret.

In general (this is not always the case), make sure that your finger is as close to the fret as possible without actually touching the fret. This will ensure that the string does not buzz or sound muffled when played.

3. One finger per string.

Be sure that only one finger touches each string. Often times you will find one finger slightly touching a neighboring string. This is particularly common with the more difficult chords (like the G major chord). This is one other cause of muffled or buzzing strings. Take some time after constructing the chord to make sure that each finger is only touching the necessary strings and not resting on neighboring strings.

4. Relax.

Relax your hand so that it is comfortable when constructing the chord. Re-position your wrist for each chord so that you are comfortable and so that your fingers can sustain their position (without cramping) while you strum.

On the following pages you will find pictures and **videos** (contained on the DVD) that explain the finger placement for 3 chords: A major, G major, and D major

These are three of the most widely used chords in popular songs today.

By learning to play **just these three chords** you will know the building blocks of many popular songs by some of the biggest recording artists.

Look at each chord diagram closely. Spend some time positioning your fingers to look like the images. Try constructing these chords yourself, strumming them, and listening to how they sound.

If you are having trouble, don't panic. Just play the **chord videos** on the DVD to watch an instructor construct the chords step by step.

Figure 13 illustrates how we number each finger when explaining how to construct chords.

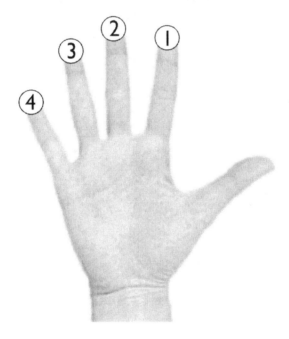

Figure 13

A Major

VIDEO: *watch Video 1 "A Major Chord"*

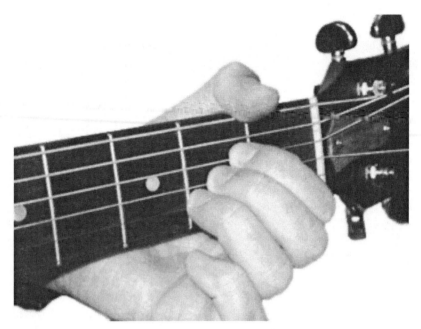

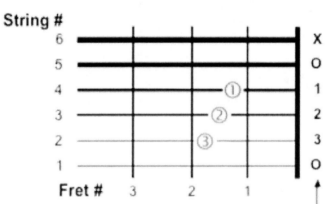

O = play these strings open

X = do not play these strings

20

G Major

VIDEO: *watch Video 2 "G Major Chord"*

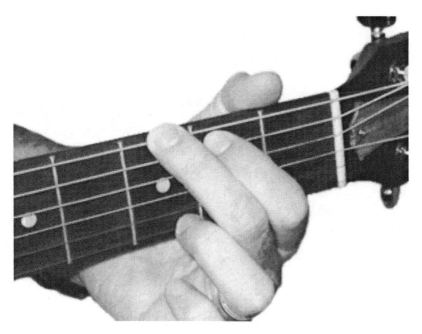

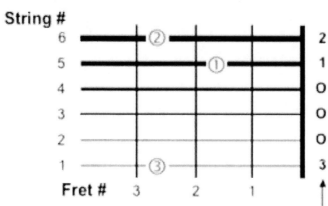

O = play these strings open

X = do not play these strings

D Major

VIDEO: *watch Video 3 "D Major Chord"*

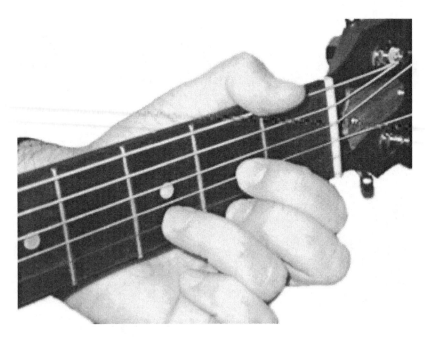

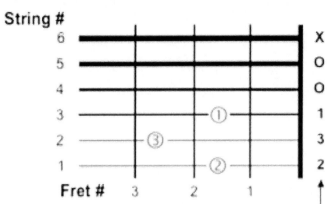

O = play these strings open

X = do not play these strings

22

6. Strumming Patterns

Now that you are comfortable with A major, D major, and G major, it's time to start making music. There are **three fundamentals** you will need in order to play songs:

1. Chord construction (which we just covered)

2. Strumming patterns

3. Transitions

Knowing the chords is the first step in playing music. If you're right handed, you use your **left hand** to construct chords and your **right hand** to strum the guitar. When you strum chords, you play the strings of your guitar with your picking hand either with a down stroke or an up stroke. **Strumming patterns** are combinations of down and up strokes that make rhythmic sense. Here are the **basic rules** to remember when strumming the guitar:

1. **Don't break your wrist.** When strumming the guitar, over 90% of the motion in your right arm should be in twisting your forearm, not breaking your wrist. Your wrist should remain firm and not flimsy. If your wrist is flimsy, your strumming will sound sloppy. Most of the up-down motion of your hand should be controlled by turning your entire forearm. Use your elbow to help your forearm move up and down.

2. **Maintain a firm grip on the pick.** Make sure that you grasp the pick firmly, or else you will not be able to generate a nice tone from the guitar. Refer back to section 4 for a refresher on proper pick technique.

3. **Your arm is a windshield wiper.** Visually, you should think of your arm as a windshield wiper that is moving up and down at the same pace, over and over. Don't ever stop your arm from moving up and down. Keep a nice rhythm. The key is to only play the up and down strokes when you want to generate sound but to always keep your arm moving up and down at a constant and steady rhythm, just like a windshield wiper.

In this section

you will learn how to play <u>two popular strumming patterns</u>.

A **strumming pattern** consists of up strokes and down strokes.

An **up stroke** is played by strumming the guitar strings from the bottom of the guitar to the top – or from the 1st (high E) string to the 6th (low E) string. We will represent an up stroke with an up arrow:

A **down stroke** is played by strumming the guitar strings from the top of the guitar to the bottom – or from the 6th (low E) string to the 1st (high E) string. We will represent a down stroke with a down arrow.

Remember to think of your strumming hand as a windshield wiper, or a pendulum. **A dashed arrow** will represent the direction your arm should be moving as you swing your arm up and down without hitting the strings.

If you need further instruction or these concepts seem a bit confusing, please read on and then make sure to watch the videos at the end of this section for an in-depth explanation from the instructor.

With just the following **two strumming patterns** you will have the ability to play many popular songs. Let's get started.

Strumming pattern one

is a very classic strumming pattern that can be used to play a number of songs.

Strumming pattern : Down, Down, up, up, down, up.

Try strumming pattern one with any of the three chords you've already learned.

If you need further instruction on strumming pattern one, please watch the video for an explanation from the instructor.

VIDEO: *watch Video 4 "Strumming Pattern 1"*

Strumming pattern two

Strumming pattern two is a slight variation on strumming pattern one, because it adds one up stroke and introduces a "swing" feel to the pattern.

Strumming pattern : Down, up, down, up, up, down, up.

(SWING)

Again, try strumming pattern two with any of the three chords you've already learned.

VIDEO: *watch Video 5 "Strumming Pattern 2"*

7. Transitions

Now you know how to play two strumming patterns with just one chord. The next step is to play these strumming patterns while transitioning **between chords**.

The most important thing to remember when learning how to transition between chords is to start out SLOWLY.

Try playing a few down strokes with the A chord and then switch to the G chord. Try to keep your strumming arm moving at a constant rhythm as you transition between chords. Slow down as much as you need to in order to ensure that your strumming arm never skips a beat. Even if it feels painfully slow, this is the only way to become proficient at changing between chords.

Another very important thing to remember is to keep your strumming arm moving at a constant, steady motion, just like a windshield wiper. You'll be amazed at how quickly you can increase the speed (or tempo) of your strumming arm if you start slowly and build up.

The trick to making transitions sound smooth is to play some open high strings or muted strings as you make your transition from one chord to another. **This ensures** that you maintain the rhythmic sound of the strumming pattern as you transition between chords. For a more in depth explanation of this transition trick, **watch the videos** on the DVD to learn from the instructor:

VIDEO: *watch Video 6 "Chord Transitions"*
             watch Video 7 "Practicing Chords"

It's important to work on keeping rhythm and tempo as you play strumming patterns and transition between chords. Remember to start slowly. Don't try to go really fast until you are totally comfortable at a slower tempo. Work your way up to a comfortable speed. You'll soon find that with just a little practice you'll be playing at any speed you want with any chords and strumming patterns. Eventually you'll even start coming up with your own patterns!

8. Practice tips

There are two important things to remember when you practice your guitar:

1. Start slowly.

Remember not to rush when you learn something new. It is always tempting to try to start playing a new chord or strumming pattern at full speed, because you are excited and want to hear it the way it is supposed to sound. If you slow down and spend an hour or so nailing the chord construction, strumming pattern, and transitions, you will have that song under your belt for the rest of your life. Conversely, if you try to play it at full speed right away and get frustrated, you may never learn it.

2. Play with a metronome.

If possible, always have a metronome with you when you practice. A metronome is a device that plays a "click" sound to the tempo (or speed) that you specify. Practice your transitions and strumming patterns to the beat of a metronome. That way you will develop some **discipline** around maintaining the "windshield wiper" rhythm with your strumming arm. Set the metronome to a slow tempo at first and then gradually increase the tempo until you are up to speed.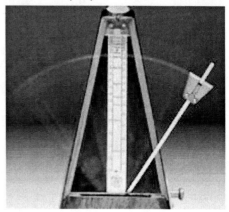

If you remember those two important rules, you will have **productive practice sessions**, and you'll be playing like a pro sooner than you can imagine.

This approach may seem slow and methodical, but it is **amazing how quickly you can** get up to speed if you start slowly. It is an exponential increase – suddenly, one day you can play fast. It seems to happen overnight!

Your **fingers** are going to hurt when you first start playing.

This is actually a good sign, and eventually you will develop hard calluses that keep the tips of your fingers protected. This can take a little time, but we recommend playing until your fingers start to get uncomfortable. When this happens take a break. There is no need to over stimulate your finger tips, so just take your time. The pain will go away and you will eventually find that you will be able to play for longer and longer periods of time with no pain at all.

Your **hands**, especially the hand you use to construct chords, may also get sore.

This is very normal. To strengthen your hand we recommend that you **watch** the video that explains how to strengthen your left hand.

VIDEO: *watch Video 8 "Finger Strength"*

Remember to **set a time every day** for practice.

Even if it's only 15 minutes. This is enough time to develop "**muscle memory**." Eventually your hands will just know what to do. It's a strange phenomenon, but the more you practice, the more you start remembering with your hands instead of your brain. When you get to this point, playing becomes really fun!

9. Songs

Well, you did it!

You've learned enough to **start playing** the songs you love. You will now be able to wow your friends, family and loved ones.

Following are a couple songs that use the chords we have taught you above – A Major, G Major, and D Major.

By combining both the chords in the right order (arrangement) and the strumming patterns you've learned, you will soon start recognizing that you are playing some very popular songs that everyone knows.

We recommend that when you are first learning these songs to buy the song and listen to it while you have your guitar in hand. Listen to the song and start to play along with it. This will help you to understand the chord progression and hear how the artists play it.

We also recommend that you **look at the chord charts** for the song. These are available for free on several internet sites, including Fretplay.com (http://www.fretplay.com/).

By looking at the chord charts, **you can see** how the chords change along with the lyrics to the song. As you listen to the song, you can follow along with the chord changes, so you know when to transition between chords.

First Song:

What I got
Sublime

This is a fun party song released in the early 90's that everyone loves. The chord progression is really simple – D Major to G Major with strumming pattern one. It just repeats D to G over and over. It's that easy!

You can **view the chord chart** on the internet at the following link:

http://www.fretplay.com/tabs/s/sublime/what_i_got-crd.shtml

Second Song:

Margaritaville
Jimmy Buffet

This is another great song to play at parties. It uses all three of the chords we've learned. You can play it with strumming pattern two, and it sounds great! It starts with the D major chord and then transitions to A Major during the verse. The chorus starts with G major and then transitions to A and D. Again, listening to this song while looking at the chord chart will help you to learn the arrangement and transitions.

You can **view the chord chart** on the internet at the following link:

http://www.fretplay.com/tabs/b/buffett_jimmy/margaritaville-crd.shtml

So now that you know the basics and have a couple popular songs under your belt, it's time to check out these **bonus videos** on the DVD to learn some more chords, cool guitar riffs, and fun chord progressions – take your playing to the next level!

VIDEO: *watch Video 9 "C Major Chord"*
watch Video 10 "A Minor Chord"
watch Video 11 "E Minor Chord"
watch Video 12 "Making Music (half speed)"
watch Video 13 "Making Music"
watch Video 14 "Riff 1"
watch Video 15 "Riff 2"
watch Video 16 "GCD Jam"

Beginner Guitar Volume 2: Styles

Rock, Blues, Country, Metal and Punk

1. Bar Chords

VIDEO: *watch Video 1 "Warm Up"*

Bar chords open up a whole new world of possibilities. Once you learn the basic bar chord shapes, you will know how to play many chords in many different positions on the neck, because bar chords sound great **no matter where** you play them.

Bar chord one

uses the entire fret board, all six strings. In constructing these types of chords, you will press down on multiple strings with just one finger. This technique of pressing down on multiple strings with one finger is called "barring."

To construct bar chord one, follow these **7 steps**:

1. Lay your **first finger**, your index finger, across all the strings (strings 6 through 1) on the third fret and press down firmly across the entire fret board.

2. **Play** the strings one at a time to make sure that the strings are not buzzing against the frets, and that all the strings are ringing out.

3. Place your **second finger** on the third string fourth fret.

4. Place your **third finger** on the fifth string fifth fret.

5. Place your **fourth finger** on the fourth string fifth fret.

6. **Play** each individual string again and make sure that each string rings out and you don't hear any fret buzz.

7. **Practice** playing this chord with strumming pattern one (from the *Volume 1* lessons).

If at any time you are getting frustrated, don't get discouraged. Take each of these steps, **one at a time**, have patience, **practice** slowly, and gradually build up strength in your hand to play this chord. Remember to practice the finger strength exercise from *Volume 1*. This will help you to build strength and coordination in both your right and left hands.

In **figure 1**, you see the shape of the bar chord.   Notice that the first finger is pressing firmly across all the strings.

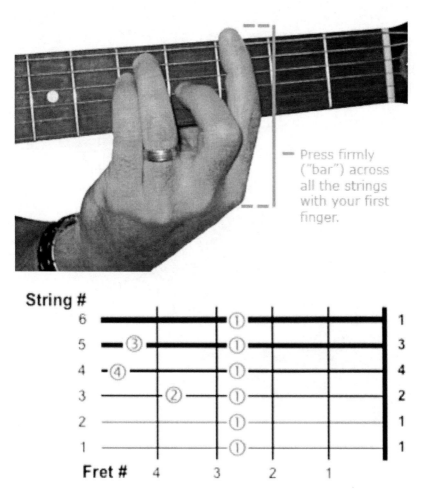

Figure 1

One of the most challenging aspects of this chord for most beginners is barring across all six stings and pressing down firmly enough, so that all the strings ring out, and you don't hear any fret buzz. The key to getting a **nice full sound** is to use your **thumb** to press firmly into the back of the neck against your first finger, so that all the strings ring out and sound good. As you are building this chord, your hand may get tired from the constant pressure that you must apply with your first finger in order to get a nice full sound. Remember to take breaks and build up slowly. This chord requires **hand strength**, which you are gradually building.

Press firmly with your thumb into the back of the neck.

Figure 2

VIDEO: *watch Video 2 "Bar Chord 1"*

Bar chord two

is a different shape than bar chord one. With this chord you will bar with your first finger **and** your third finger.

To construct bar chord one, follow these **6 steps**:

1. Lay your **first finger**, your index finger, across strings 5 through 1 on the third fret and press down firmly across the fret board.

2. **Play** the strings one at a time to make sure that the frets are not buzzing, and that all the strings are ringing out.

3. Lay your **third finger** across strings 4, 3, and 2 on the fifth fret.

4. **Play** each individual string again and make sure that each string rings out and you don't hear any fret buzz.

5. **Practice** playing this chord with strumming pattern one (from the *Volume 1* lessons).

6. Make sure you do not play the sixth string.

In **figure 3**, you see the shape of the bar chord.   Notice how you bar with both the first and the third fingers.

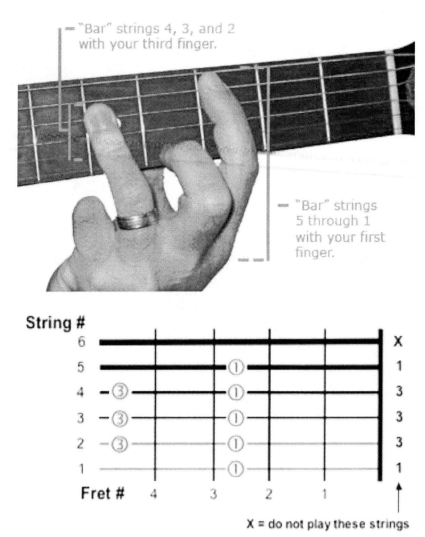

Figure 3

VIDEO: *watch Video 3 "Bar Chord 2"*

Moving Bar Chords Around

The beauty of bar chords is that once you have learned the basic shape, you can move this same shape **up and down the neck**, and it sounds great no matter where you play it.

Try moving both **Bar Chord 1** and **Bar Chord 2** up and down the neck, and notice that they both sound good no matter where you play them.

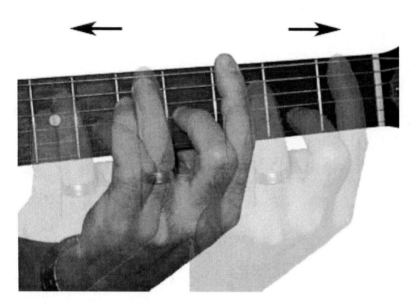

Figure 4

Special note: The two bar chords we have just learned are **major** bar chords. As you move them up and down the neck, what you are doing is playing a different major chord each time. Here are some examples of the names of the chords you are playing as you move your hand up and down the neck:

Bar Chord 1

First finger is on the...	Name of the chord is...
First fret ------------------▶	F Major
Third fret ----------------▶	G Major
Fifth fret ------------------▶	A Major

Bar Chord 2

First finger is on the...	Name of the chord is...
Second fret ------------------▶	B Major
Third fret ------------------▶	C Major
Fifth fret ------------------▶	D Major

2. Styles

The rest of this book is dedicated to teaching you different styles of playing guitar. We chose **rock, blues, country, and metal and punk,** because these apply well to the guitar, and you often hear elements of these different styles mixed together, even within the same song. Rock is based on blues; metal and punk are based on rock; and country and folk elements are at the heart of **a countless number of popular songs** that incorporate blues, rock, and even metal and punk styles. So, even if you only love one of these four genres, it is well worth it to learn something about each of them, because music and songs are **melting pots** of ideas, often crossing over genres and boundaries.

In the following sections, **the videos will become much more important** for your learning, because for each style, we have created a step-by-step sequence of videos that, in combination with this book, are designed to get you playing the "jams" as quickly as possible.

You should **approach** each of these sections as follows:

1. **Scan once** quickly through the section and pick up what you can.

2. Make sure to **watch** any new chord **videos** for that section that you will need to learn before the first strumming video.

3. **Watch** the first strumming **video** and play along.

4. **Return** to the book and read through the explanation of the strumming pattern once more.

5. **Watch** the strumming **video** again.

6. **Watch** the transition **video**.

7. **Practice** transitioning between chords with the new strumming pattern.

8. When you have practiced and you feel comfortable, watch the "jam" video and **jam along** with the instructor.

Rhythm and "Feel"

Rhythm and "feel" is something that you really need to see and hear in order to fully grasp. For that reason, we strongly recommend that you **watch the videos** to learn how each strumming pattern within each style should be played. We've tried to explain rhythm and feel as best as we can in writing, but if you find you're having trouble understanding this material, the videos will allow you to **see and hear** the rhythm, which for some people is a much more intuitive way to learn.

Our approach to teaching rhythm and feel in words is to use **numbers and your own voice**. Each style has it's own signature rhythm or "feel" that makes it easy to recognize. In describing this typical feel for each style, we've listed the numbers 1 2 3 4 under the title of each section. This indicates which beats are emphasized in a four-beat pattern.

Count out loud "one, two, three, four" at a steady tempo over and over, and then say a number louder or softer depending on these rules:

1. When a number is <u>underlined</u> that means it should be emphasized (say it louder).

2. When a number is **bold** *and* <u>underlined</u> that means it should be **really** emphasized (say it really loud).

This 1 2 3 4 rhythm and feel guideline is listed below each style title as well as under the arrows that describe each strumming pattern. Try to emphasize or de-emphasize the up and down strokes for each strumming pattern depending on what the recommended feel is.

Special Note: In *Volume 1* you were first introduced to the concept of strumming patterns. Following is a refresher on some of the terminology and symbols used in this book to describe strumming patterns:

> A **strumming pattern** consists of up strokes and down strokes.

An **up stroke** is played by strumming the guitar strings from the bottom of the guitar to the top – or from the 1st (high E) string to the 6th (low E) string. We will represent an up stroke with an up arrow:

A **down stroke** is played by strumming the guitar strings from the top of the guitar to the bottom – or from the 6th (low E) string to the 1st (high E) string. We will represent a down stroke with a down arrow.

Remember to think of your strumming hand as a windshield wiper, or a pendulum. **A dashed arrow** will represent the direction your arm should be moving as you swing your arm up and down without hitting the strings.

If arrows are spaced equally apart from each other, then you will keep your strumming hand moving up and down in a steady, even motion.

If arrows are spaced closer together and further apart, such as with a pattern that has a **swing** feel, try adjusting your arm swing to give the pattern a swing feel (if you have difficulty swinging the pattern just by reading the book, make sure to **watch the videos** first).

3. Rock

New Chords

F Major

VIDEO: *watch Video 4 "F Major Chord"*

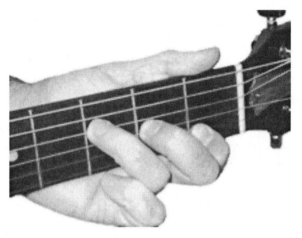

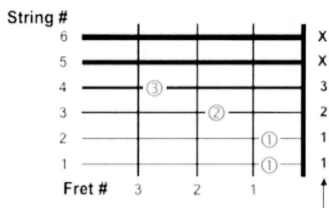

O = play these strings open

X = do not play these strings

Figure 5

42

Rock lesson one

CHORDS USED IN THIS LESSON:

- C Major (taught in *Volume 1*)
- F Major

Rock rhythms are typically more "straight ahead." This means that that in a four-beat pattern, you will typically balance the emphasis on the 1 and the 3. **Practice** saying out loud "one, two, three, four," saying "one" and "three" louder and putting an equal **emphasis** on the "one" and the "three."

Notice how in the first half of the strumming pattern (the section before the dotted line), the down strokes clearly emphasize the 1 and the 3. In the second half, however, you do not play the first down stroke, but it is "implied" that this is where the emphasis is. If this is not totally clear, don't worry. That's why we use the word "feel" to describe how a rhythm should be played, because sometimes it can't be described perfectly with logic. Make sure to **watch the video** and play along with the instructor if at any point this seems unclear.

Strumming pattern: Down, Down, up, down, down, up, up, down, up, down.

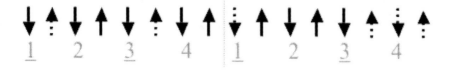

Once you've mastered rock strumming pattern one, it's time to move on to the transition. Make sure to nail the F Major chord, the strumming pattern, and the transition, before playing along with the jam video.

VIDEO: *watch Video 5 "Rock Strumming 1"*
watch Video 6 "Rock Transition 1"
watch Video 7 "Rock Jam 1"

4. Blues

1 2 **3** 4

New Chords

A7

VIDEO: *watch Video 8 "A7 Chord"*

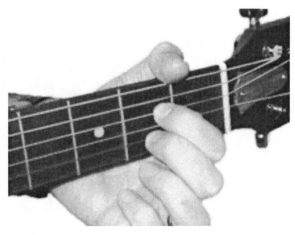

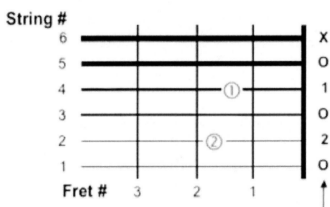

O = play these strings open

X = do not play these strings

Figure 7

D7

VIDEO: *watch Video 9 "D7 Chord"*

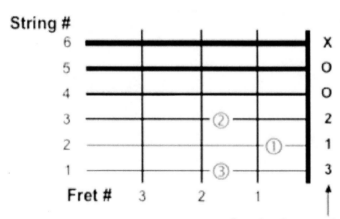

Figure 8

E Major

VIDEO: *watch Video 10 "E Major Chord"*

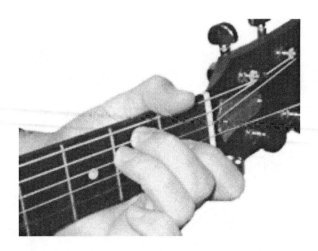

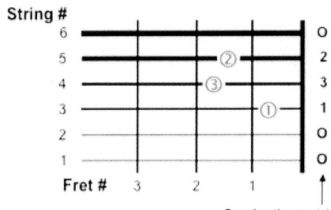

Figure 9

E7

VIDEO: *watch Video 11 "E7"*

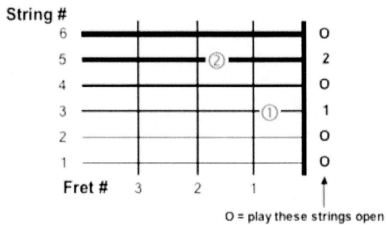

O = play these strings open

X = do not play these strings

Figure 10

Blues lesson one

CHORDS USED IN THIS LESSON:

- A7
- D7
- E7

Blues rhythms typically have a pretty heavy emphasis on beat 3. Try counting out loud while emphasizing beat 3. Notice how you may have a tendency to **slow down** the tempo. Blues songs are often emotional and have slower tempos, and for some reason, emphasizing beat 3 at slower tempos feels more natural.

Swing

Blues strumming pattern one also has a nice swing feel. What do we mean by "swing" feel?

For a minute, try counting out loud "one, two, three, four" slowly at a steady tempo. Now add the word "and" between each number as you count out loud. So you'll count out "one, **and**, two, **and**, three, **and** four **and**, one, **and**...." After you feel comfortable adding the word "and" between each number, try delaying the "and" slightly after each number, so the "and" will lag after "one" and then push into "two," lag after "two" and push into "three," etc. If you let the "and" lag just a little bit and then push into the next beat, you'll notice that you start to feel like the rhythm is **lagging and pushing**, lagging and pushing. This lag and push feeling is a **swing feel**.

Just imagine sitting in a swing while counting "one, **and**, two, **and**, one, **and**, two, **and**..." over and over out loud. When you start out, you use your legs to hold you up in the air, and you count out "one." As you rapidly swing forward, you quickly count out "and" and then as you are suspended in air, you take a breath and count out "two." Then as you swing backwards, you quickly count out "and" before being suspended in air again when you **begin again** at "one." The idea is that as you are traveling through the air quickly you count out the "and." At the peaks when you are suspended in the air, you count out "one" and "two."

Figure 11

Swinging the rhythm while counting it out is one thing, but playing a strumming pattern on guitar with a swing feel is yet another step. After getting comfortable counting out a swing feel as "one, **and**, two, **and**, three, **and**, four, **and**...," **watch** the blues strumming pattern **video**, and get the feel for the arm motion of blues strumming pattern one.

Special note: Notice how the "&" beats below are all **up strokes,** and how these upstrokes are located a little closer to the next upcoming down stroke, indicating the "lag" and "push" swing feel.

Strumming pattern : Down, Down, down, up, up, down, down.

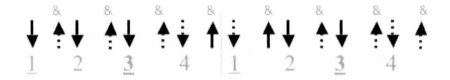

Just like with rock strumming pattern one, in the first half of the strumming pattern (the section before the dotted line) the down strokes clearly emphasize the 1 and, especially, the 3. In the second half, however, you do not play the first down stroke, but again it is "implied" that this is where the emphasis is.

Special note: Are you noticing a trend here? What's happening is that often to keep strumming patterns interesting, artists will use a **"call and response"** technique, where the first half of a pattern is fairly straightforward, and the second half is a "response" or variation on the first half. Even though the second half of the pattern may be different than the first half to add variation, the overall **feel** of the pattern is still the same. In this case, the bluesy swing feel is still strong, even though there is a variation in the response half of the pattern.

VIDEO: *watch Video 12 "Blues Strumming 1"*
watch Video 13 "Blues Transition 1"
watch Video 14 "Blues Jam 1"

5. Country/Folk

1 2 3 4

Country lesson one

CHORDS USED IN THIS LESSON:

- A Minor (taught in *Volume 1*)
- C Major (taught in *Volume 1*)
- F Major
- G Major (taught in *Volume 1*)

In country songs, the guitarist's emphasis on beats 2 and 4 makes you want to get up and dance. Country drummers will often play the bass drum on beats 1 and 3 to add emphasis to the **bass line** in the song. It's the guitarist's job to **follow along** with the bass, but emphasize beats 2 and 4 in order to give the music an "up tempo" feel.

One technique to achieve this is to play along with the bass line on 1 and 3, but **emphasize** 2 and 4. The rhythm guitarist may play individual "bass," or low sounding, notes on the guitar in order to follow along with the drummer and bass player, but strum chords on 2 and 4 in order to keep the dance floor hoppin'!

Special note: Country strumming pattern one also has a swing feel. For a refresher on swing, re-read the Blues section, which explains how to treat the "&" strokes in the pattern below.

Strumming pattern: Down, Down, up, down, down, up

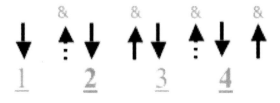

51

Make sure to nail all the chords, the strumming pattern, and the transition, before playing along with the jam video.

VIDEO: *Watch Video 15 "Country Strumming 1"*
Watch Video 16 "Country Transition 1"
Watch Video 17 "Country Jam 1"

6. Metal and Punk

Power Chords

Power chords are the standard weapons of choice among metal and punk guitarists. Just like bar chords, power chords have the characteristic of sounding good **no matter where** you position them on the guitar neck. Once you learn the basic power chord shape, you can move it **up and down the neck**, and it sounds good no matter where you play it.

In **figures 12** and **13**, you see the shape and construction of power chords 1 and 2 using three fingers. Just like bar chords, power chord shapes can be moved up and down the neck, and they sound great. You can think of these as "stripped down" versions of bar chords. The 3-finger versions are **just the first three notes** (the top section) of a bar chord shape. NOTE: this chord can also be played with just fingers 1 and 3. There are a few reasons why these chords are used a lot in metal and punk:

- You can play them **fast**
- You can play them **hard**
- You can play them with lots of **distortion** and they sound great (on electric guitar)

Power Chord 1 (3 Fingers)

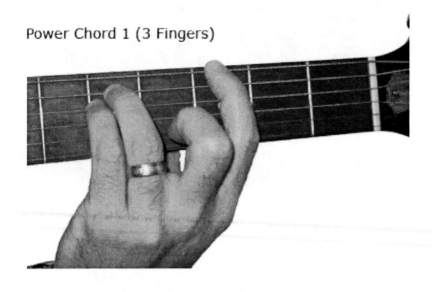

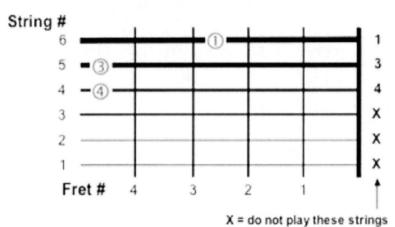

String #

6			①		1
5	③				3
4	④				4
3					X
2					X
1					X

Fret #   4   3   2   1

X = do not play these strings

Figure 12

Power Chord 2 (3 Fingers)

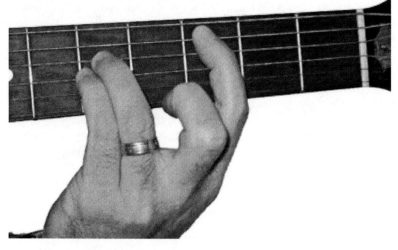

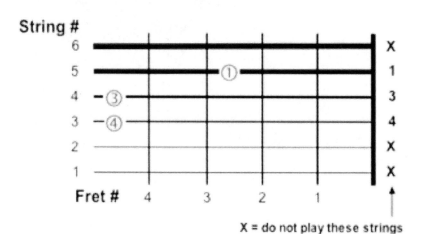

X = do not play these strings

Figure 13

55

Muting

In strumming a power chord, you have two basic options: play it muted, or play it open.

Muting is a technique in which you lay the side of your strumming hand across the strings near the bridge of the guitar, and then strum the guitar while maintaining your hand position.

Figures 14 and **15** illustrate how you mute the strings while strumming with the same hand. Playing muted power chords is common in many genres of music, and it is perhaps most predominant in metal, although it is used quite a bit in punk as well. If you are looking for a "chunky" sound that is extremely **rhythmic and precise**, then muting is a great way to do that.

Lay the side of your hand across the strings, as near as possible to the bridge.

Figure 14

Strum with side/palm of your hand laying across ("muting") the strings.

Figure 15

The other option in playing power chords is to play them **open** rather than muting them. This sound is more common in punk, where the precision that you can achieve with muting is not as important. If you are looking for a hard, thrashy slightly disorganized sound, then open power chords might be the right choice.

VIDEO: *watch Video 20 "Power Chord 1"*
            watch Video 21 "Muting Power Chord 1"
            watch Video 22 "Power Chord 2"

Metal and punk lesson one

CHORDS USED IN THIS LESSON:

- Power Chord 1
- Power Chord 2

Much of the **feel** of music has to do with the **mood** that you are trying to convey. In rock, the steady rhythm makes for great driving music. In blues, the emphasis on the third beat works well with slower tempos and moodier lyrical content. In country, the juxtaposition of downbeats and upbeats makes people want to tap their fingers or get up and dance.

In metal and punk, there is often a very strong emphasis on beat 1. If you count "one, two, three, four" over and over out loud, **emphasizing** the 1, you'll notice that it starts to sound like a battle chant, or you might imagine that you're an angry drill sergeant commanding a march or a quarterback barking out plays. By emphasizing beat 1, the music definitely starts to feel aggressive, and this isn't surprising, since many metal and punk songs use aggression to get a point across.

Strumming pattern: Down, Down, down, down

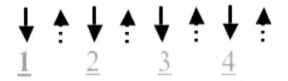

Once you've mastered metal strumming pattern one, it's time to move on to the transitions. Make sure to nail the muting technique, all the chords, the strumming pattern, and the transitions, before playing along with the jam video.

VIDEO: watch Video 21 "Metal Strumming 1"
watch Video 22 "Metal Transition 1"
watch Video 23 "Metal Transition 2"
watch Video 24 "Metal Jam 1"

7. Songs

If you haven't already purchased music **through Apple's iTunes Music Store**, we recommend that you download the latest version of iTunes and try it out: http://www.apple.com/itunes/. This is an incredible resource for finding and listening to music. You can buy an individual song and then play along with it, using the new skills you've learned through these lessons. Each song costs just .99 cents, and if you only need one song and not the entire album, this is the perfect choice.

If you don't already own the following songs, go to iTunes and purchase them, because they use the techniques that we've taught you here in *Volume 2*:

> *The First Cut is the Deepest,* **Sheryl Crow**
> *Farther on Down the Road,* **Taj Mahal**
> *On the Road Again*, **Willie Nelson**
> *Come Out and Play*, **The Offspring**

Rock Song:

The First Cut is the Deepest
Sheryl Crow

This is a great example of a classic, "straight ahead" feeling rock song. Try using rock strumming pattern one in combination with the chords D Major, A Major, and G Major. Change chords as indicated in the pattern below:

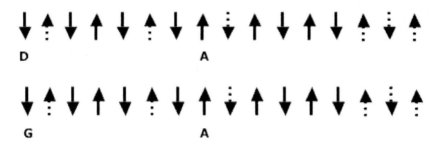

REPEAT

Blues Song:

Farther on Down the Road
Taj Mahal

Try playing blues strumming pattern one alternating between the A7 and D7 chords, and you'll be amazed out how good it sounds! Change chords as indicated in the pattern below:

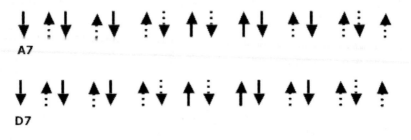

A7

D7

REPEAT

Country Song:

On the Road Again
Willie Nelson

This tune is a perfect example of country strumming pattern one in action. There are quite a few chord changes, and the tempo is fast, but if you practice it slowly you'll get it! You can play this song with E Major, Bar Chord 1 (4th fret), Power Chord 1 (2nd fret), A Major, and Bar Chord 2 (2nd fret). Play each chord with country strumming pattern one the following number of times:

    E Major **8** times
    ...then Bar Chord 1 (4th fret) **8** times
    ...then Power Chord 1 (2nd fret) **4** times,
    ...then A Major **2** times
    ...then Bar Chord 2 (2nd fret) **2** times
    ...then E Major **8** times

    REPEAT

Metal/Punk Song:

Come out and Play
The Offspring

Use Power Chord 1 and 2 with the muting technique to play this song. Change chords as indicated in the pattern below:

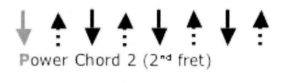

Power Chord 2 (2nd fret)

PC 1 (2nd fret)   PC 1 (5th fret)

REPEAT

8. Chords

Bar Chord 1

VIDEO: watch Video 2 *"Bar Chord 1"*

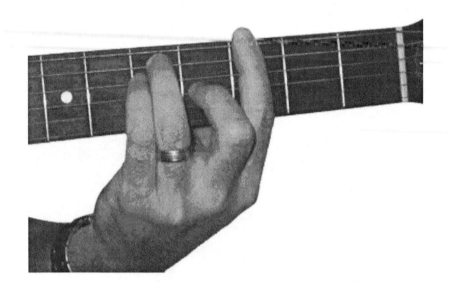

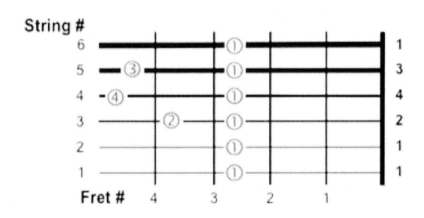

Figure 16

Bar Chord 2

VIDEO: *watch Video 3 "Bar Chord 2"*

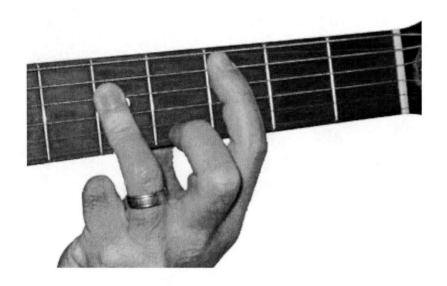

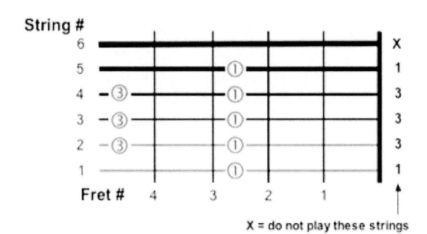

Figure 17

F Major

VIDEO: *watch Video 4 "F Major Chord"*

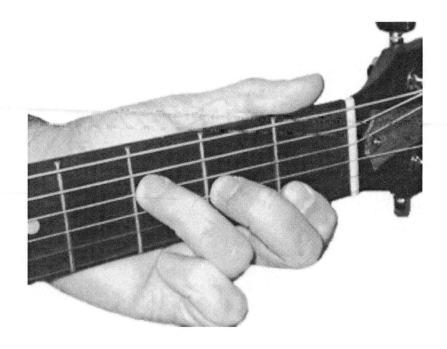

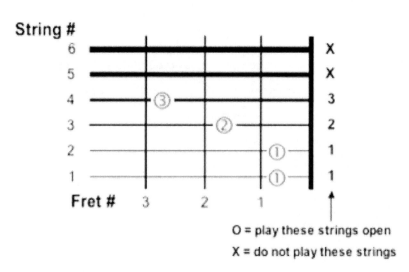

O = play these strings open

X = do not play these strings

Figure 18

A7

VIDEO: *watch Video 8 "A7 Chord"*

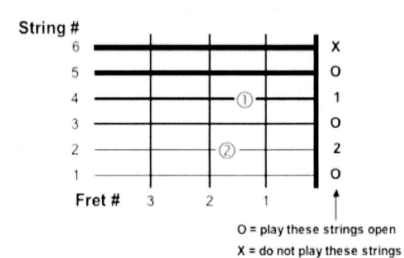

O = play these strings open

X = do not play these strings

Figure 19

D7

VIDEO: *watch Video 9 "D7 Chord"*

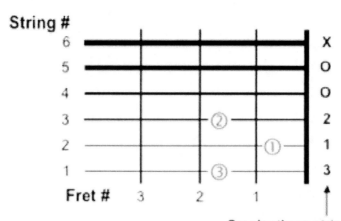

Figure 20

E Major

VIDEO: *watch Video 10 "E Major Chord"*

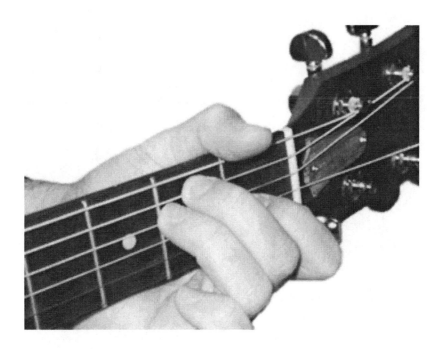

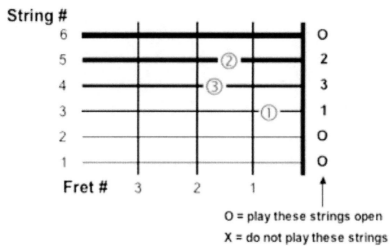

Figure 21

E7

VIDEO: *watch Video 11 "E7"*

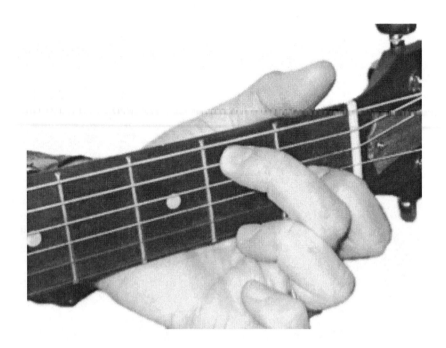

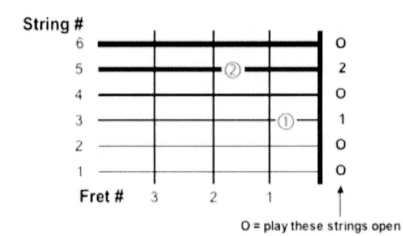

O = play these strings open

X = do not play these strings

Figure 22

Power Chord 1

VIDEO: *watch Video 18 "Power Chord 1"*

Power Chord 1 (3 Fingers)

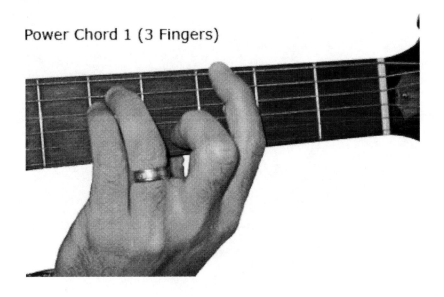

NOTE: this chord can also be played with just fingers 1 and 3.

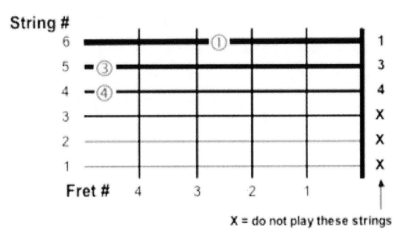

X = do not play these strings

Figure 23

Power Chord 2

VIDEO: *watch Video 20 "Power Chord 2"*

Power Chord 2 (3 Fingers)

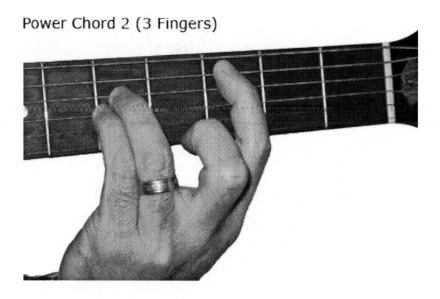

NOTE: this chord can also be played with just fingers 1 and 3.

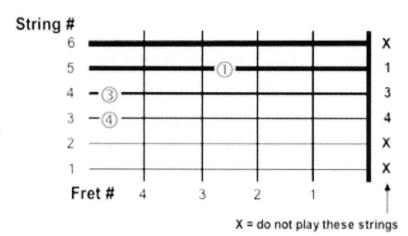

X = do not play these strings

Figure 24

70

9. Next Steps

So now that you know how to play some rock, blues, country, metal and punk songs, it's time to check out the **bonus videos**, which will give you even more chords, cool guitar riffs, and fun progressions to play around with.

VIDEO: watch Video 25 *"Riff 1 Expanded"*
watch Video 26 *"Riff 3 – Rock"*
watch Video 27 *"Riff 4 – Mellow"*
watch Video 28 *"D Minor Chord"*
watch Video 29 *"G7 Chord"*

We also recommend that you **visit** the Harmony Central website. You can get there by clicking on the following URL –

http://www.harmonycentral.com/

When you get to the site, click on the "Tablature" link

http://www.harmony-central.com/Guitar/tab.html

Tablature, or "tab," is very useful for learning popular songs. It is a type of musical notation that is very easy to understand for those of us that can't read music. The Tablature page on Harmony Central has several links that you can click on to learn how to read tab.

After you understand how to read tab, you can **browse** the OLGA database for songs that you want to learn how to play. It's very easy so don't get frustrated.   In fact, you don't really even need to understand tab to take advantage of the files in the OLGA database, because most of them show the chord changes as well, so you can just use them as simple chord charts.   Just play the chord that is above the lyric and change it when a new chord name appears. It's very easy and fun. You can browse by artist and find free tablature for all your favorite songs.

We would also recommend going to any major online or bricks-and-mortar guitar stores such as Guitar Center or Sweetwater.com and buying books, tapes and videos. There are some great tools out there for learning more songs, scales, theory and technique.

Finally, remember to check back at our website often:

http://www.iPlayMusic.com

We are working hard right now to develop more song-based videos and learning materials to help you learn more popular songs and develop more advanced techniques. Stay tuned for many more exciting products to come!

Thank you for purchasing *Beginner Guitar Lessons* from iPlayMusic. On behalf of the entire iPlayMusic team, we wish you success in your newfound passion! We would love to hear from you and value **your feedback**. Please send us your comments and any ideas you might have for additional instructional tools and videos:

feedback@iplaymusic.com